WALL STREET JO

s News—

*120 Significant
Things Men
Know...but Never
Ask About*

BAKER
A DIVISION OF
Baker Book House Co

FINGERTIP BOOKS

Copyright 1994 by John Leax

Published by Baker Books
a division of Baker Book House Company
P.O. Box 6287, Grand Rapids, MI 49516-6287

ISBN: 0-8010-5694-2

Printed in the United States of America

A sentence is like a knife:
a dull one endangers
the craftsman.

$\mathcal{T}$he impossibility
of perfect purity is no
excuse for promiscuity.

I've never met an economy that didn't oppress someone.

~

*C*ommunity can be either good or bad; it can't be avoided.

$\mathcal{T}$he strongest argument for an afterlife is the wild extravagance of God evidenced in creation.

The success of our consumer culture depends on people loving money more than life.

A cardinal's feathers are softer than a starling's; God loves them equally.

~

Some desire faith to move mountains; in this age of bulldozers we need faith to keep them in place.

A big fish in a small pond will eventually starve.

~

A man planting trees in rows has designs on nature.

*Even forgiven sins
have consequences.*

~

*Grace always
offends justice.*

The dreams of idealists
often turn into the
nightmares of realists.

~

Christ died because he
had no illusions about
human nature.

The turtle sees more than the hare.

$\mathcal{I}$n the honest heart faith
and doubt are not rivals.

$\mathcal{M}$any wish to see God;
few wish to be seen by him.

If I do not deliberately choose to be a friend of the powerless, I become by default an ally of the powerful.

Only that faith given by grace, achieved by the groaning of the Holy Spirit within us, is faith sufficient to sustain us in times of trial and suffering.

All morality is public morality.

~

Salvation is not earned by passing a vocabulary quiz.

*I*n the face of grief
human empathy
is more comforting than
theological truth.

Anyone who doubts the efficacy of the word should remember God spoke the world into being.

Success often results
from nothing more noble
than the fear of being
thought a failure.

~

When the end of
knowledge is power,
ignorance is bliss.

One does not need to live long into adulthood before a learned distrust of social institutions overcomes a healthy suspicion of individualism.

The voracious evil of impersonal bureaucracies could not exist without the wholehearted participation of good men.

$\mathcal{A}$ leader must choose:
he may seek to bring about
the will of the people or the
good of the people.
One leads to chaos,
the other to tragedy.

Solar energy will release us from our dependency on coal, oil, and nuclear power as soon as some corporation succeeds in establishing legal title to the sun or as soon as we learn to want no more than we need.

Though our cultural practice appears nominally Christian, our worship of money and status still requires human sacrifice.

$\mathcal{B}$oth conservatives and liberals believe the government is responsible for every social ill.

A cat on the bird feeder is not after seeds.

~

Being able to say *I'm a good man* isn't saying much.

$\mathcal{T}$he work of an economy should be the just and generous distribution of goods, not the accumulation of wealth by the strong at the expense of the weak.

$\mathcal{A}$ tyrant's first victim is
his own freedom.

The celebration of sabbath is an announcement to the world that we will be owned by no one but God.

What I don't want
I don't need.

~

Consumer culture rises
from a foundation of
wishes, lies, and dreams.

Offer a man money, sex, or power, he'll fall more often than a drunk on ice.

$\mathcal{B}$linded by approaching light, a deer cannot move; neither can a Godseeker.

The indignity of birth and death comes to everyone; the indignity of a life lived meanly comes to those who choose it.

One can learn to live with violence, corruption, and environmental degradation, or one can announce that the emperor is naked.

The church is only one
region of the
kingdom of God.

$\mathcal{A}$ ceremony, depending on the celebrants, can be an empty form or something to stand on.

The doctrine of total depravity may be true, but one would have to be totally depraved to believe it.

The inevitable discrepancy between one's ideals and one's behavior does not constitute hypocrisy.

The automobile guarantees three things: smog, suburbia, and sexually experienced teenagers.

$\mathcal{A}$ measure of character
is the ability to refuse
power.

～

$\mathcal{K}$nown truth can be
sufficient; it can never
be complete.

$\mathcal{D}$emocracy will survive only as long as individuals and families have access to usable land and knowledge to use it.

A need for admiration can never be met.

~

Good work always appears effortless.

Community begins in an
accurate dialogue with
the self.

~

Of history and myth only
one can be trusted.

The owner of a
promiscuous mouth, his
conversation is unsafe.

~

No one needs a gold
watch to measure time.

*M*any writers have
delivered books before
conceiving them.

~

A culture determined to
honor winners must first
make losers.

Unlike a healthy ego, a healthy economy is always subordinate to community.

No decade is more
selfish than the one
it precedes.

$\mathcal{N}$aming the animals, we not only define their beings, we define our responsibility and connection to them.

The nature of human beings makes a strong central government necessary, not desirable.

I'd rather have a red neck from bending to my work than the soft hands of a usurious lender.

When the civil authorities fear the conscience of a single individual, the time for revolution has arrived.

~

Every solution creates a new problem.

$\mathcal{L}$ittle difference exists between the naive optimism of a modern technocrat and the hubris of a Greek tragic hero.

The body learns to tolerate increasing doses of arsenic; the mind, on the other hand, succumbs instantly to the poison of TV.

$\mathcal{A}$ society practicing neither modesty nor restraint has no claim on a right to privacy.

No couple on the day of their wedding can comprehend the awfulness of their vows.

A high incidence of abortion testifies to a culture's lost hope.

~

Atheists and evangelists are alike; they share an intolerance of ambiguity.

Given the lives most choose to live, what is there for the honest writer to write except exposés, complaints, and laments? Stories of hope and psalms of praise.

To write aphorisms one must be opinionated, egotistical, and witty.

The idea of The City is a beautiful thing.

~

A strip-mine frog pond harbors wonders enough for a lifetime.

$\mathcal{A}$ mouse in the ceiling
suggests a house is free
of snakes.

~

$\mathcal{T}$he truth of an idea has
no relationship to its
newness.

A science that finds God irrelevant demonstrates the narrowness of its concerns.

$\mathcal{M}$any memories are
founded in fact.

∼

$\mathcal{G}$od is not diminished by
the disregard of his
creatures.

When the words *cash* and *incentive* are synonyms, labor is devalued.

*O*ne cannot understand
the Bible without
understanding the book
of nature.

Only a fool or someone enamored with his own strength splits wood against the grain.

$\mathcal{T}$hough a snake
swallowing a frog
is doing God's will,
the frog cannot be blamed
for resisting.

Salvation is being placed in right relationship with the Creator; however it may be extended, it occurs here in this world, and it exists in the present moment.

In a healthy community the right to entertain heresy does not need protection.

To be an environmentalist requires one to do more than preserve the principle of the earth's resources for long-term exploitation; it requires one to revalue the earth and reimagine the place of the human in the community of the creation.

Grackles have their own beauty, but when they take over the feeder, I stop buying seed.

In mastering a craft we proceed from flaw to flaw.

~

My salvation will be complete only when I cease to resent God's forgiveness of those who have hurt me.

A woodsplitter contributes
more to the health of a
community than a
hairsplitter.

~

A beaver does not know
his work's end is a meadow.

One of the most discouraging facts of life is how little understanding of the facts of life is necessary for two human beings to successfully reproduce themselves.

The pleasure of splitting wood comes from the necessity to look at each round and come to understand it before lifting an ax or placing a wedge; only when the grain is rightly understood will it yield to a single blow.

No committee, however distinguished its members, can demonstrate the intelligence, creativity, or integrity of a single individual, for the whole purpose of a committee is to provide the anonymity necessary to make impersonal decisions.

To find himself a man needs to go far out into his own loneliness; then he needs a woman graced with hospitality to lead him back to town.

When all things are equal,
humor is impossible.

~

Everyone wants someone
to say yes to.

$\mathcal{S}$ome Christians, eager to see their Lord, look forward to dying; theirs is a strange longing, for God is present in creation, available without the inconvenience of dying to anyone who will look.

Only victims speak of massacres and holocausts; the perpetrators of such acts speak of total victory.

~

A bird in the hand does not sing.

More people spend time making good money than making good lives; bless them, they get what they deserve.

$\mathcal{A}$ child deserves a world where a smack on the side of the head means a kiss on a cheek.

A rooster struts because
his knowledge is limited to
hens.

A rooster capable of
imagining a hatchet
would neither strut nor
crow.

$\mathcal{I}$f it weren't for
obligations, I'd never
go anywhere.

~

$\mathcal{O}$ne may swallow one's
pride, but one cannot
digest it.

Most Christians find it more worthy to go to the ends of the earth to serve Christ than to cross the street to serve their neighbor.

$\mathcal{C}$hristian environmentalism is founded on the right of God to have his creation intact.

What is most fascinating about the telephone is the compulsion to answer it.

$\mathfrak{M}$ore than the violence of society, I fear the violence of myself; the ways of peace are not natural, I must learn them.

An honest man in the political arena has about the same chances of survival as a saint in the Coliseum.

$\mathcal{A}$ talking chimpanzee would not diminish my sense of what it means to be human; it would elevate my sense of what it means to be a chimpanzee.

A drop of dew in sunlight
shines more brightly than
a freshly minted coin.

~

In the kingdom of God
there is no such thing as a
mere dandelion.

In the presence of mystery, proceed with caution.

~

Living in the world means living with mosquitoes.

A man tired of himself is unlikely to find happiness living as a recluse.

An occasional dose of loneliness is an agreeable medicine; it builds one's immunity to the trivial aggravations of friendship.

A finite being, I must parcel out my love—so much for my wife and child, my neighbors, my cat, and the fish in my pond; God, on the other hand, is not so hampered. His finite love reaches even the spider in the bath.